P9-CCG-908

THE HISTORY OF
RACISM IN AMERICA

BY DUCHESS HARRIS, JD, PHD
WITH TAMMY GAGNE

Core Library

An Imprint of Abdo Publishing
abdobooks.com

Cover image: In the early 1960s, some people protested
segregation outside of school board offices.

JUV NON FIC
305.8 HAR

abdobooks.com

Printed in the United States of America, North Mankato, Minnesota
102020
012021

THIS BOOK CONTAINS
RECYCLED MATERIALS

Cover Photo: PhotoQuest/Archive Photos/Getty Images
Interior Photos: Sean Pavone/Shutterstock Images, 4–5; Kristi Blokhin/Shutterstock Images, 9; Shutterstock Images, 10; Glasshouse Images/Newscom, 11; Library of Congress, 14–15; Everett Collection/Newscom, 16, 20, 43; Anthony Berger/Library of Congress, 18; Bettmann/Getty Images, 22–23; Alfred R. Waud/Library of Congress, 25; AP Images, 27; Everett Collection/Shutterstock Images, 28; Red Line Editorial, 29; Jessey Dearing/The Boston Globe/Getty Images, 32–33; Daniel Boczarski/Getty Images Entertainment/Getty Images, 36; John Raoux/AP Images, 39

Editor: Marie Pearson
Series Designer: Sarah Taplin

Library of Congress Control Number: 2020944096

Publisher's Cataloging-in-Publication Data

Names: Harris, Duchess, author. | Gagne, Tammy, author.
Title: The history of racism in America / by Duchess Harris and Tammy Gagne
Description: Minneapolis, Minnesota : Abdo Publishing, 2021 | Series: Core library guide to racism in modern America | Includes online resources and index
Identifiers: ISBN 9781532194641 (lib. bdg.) | ISBN 9781644945070 (pbk.) | ISBN 9781098214166 (ebook)
Subjects: LCSH: Racism--United States--History--Juvenile literature. | Race relations--Juvenile literature. | United States--History--Juvenile literature. | Prejudices--United States--Juvenile literature.
Classification: DDC 305.8--dc23

CONTENTS

A LIFE SENTENCE

On January 5, 1997, a Black man named Fair Wayne Bryant was on his way to Bossier City, Louisiana. It was after midnight. The 38-year-old got lost in the city of Shreveport. He was driving a blue van that he had borrowed from his cousin. Then the van stopped running. Bryant thought he needed gas. He began looking for a gas can. He entered the storeroom of a home's carport. A carport is an open-air shelter that people can

Shreveport is in northwestern Louisiana.

park vehicles under. The door was unlocked. But Bryant did not have permission to enter.

Charles Ray, the homeowner, saw Bryant in the carport. He called the Shreveport Police Department. He said the thief fled in a van. Officer Joseph Dews was about six blocks away. He saw a van that matched the description Ray gave. Dews stopped the vehicle. Bryant was driving it. Dews searched the vehicle. He found a pair of hedge clippers. Bryant explained that he had run out of gas. He admitted to entering Ray's storeroom. But he said he did not take the clippers. Bryant's cousin later told authorities that they belonged to him. But Ray said the garden tool was his.

Six months later, a jury convicted Bryant of attempted simple burglary. Bryant had previously served ten years of hard labor for armed robbery. It was his only violent crime. But because of his past, he received a mandatory minimum sentence of life in prison for stealing the hedge clippers. Bryant filed an appeal. He said that the sentence was excessive. But the judge upheld the verdict.

More than 20 years later, Bryant was still in prison for the crime. In August 2020 the case reached the Louisiana Supreme Court. But the court denied Bryant's request to review the case. The state had a habitual offender law. This law increases penalties the more crimes someone commits. Repeat offenders can receive life sentences even for petty crimes. Petty crimes are minor crimes.

PERSPECTIVES

THE COST OF LONG SENTENCES

Excessive punishments do not only affect the person convicted. They are also expensive for the community. Chief Justice Bernette J. Johnson of the Louisiana Supreme Court pointed out how much money the state of Louisiana could spend to keep Bryant in prison for life. By 2020 he had already spent almost 23 years in prison. "If he lives another 20 years," she wrote, "Louisiana taxpayers will have paid almost one million dollars to punish Mr. Bryant for his failed effort to steal a set of hedge clippers."

They include stealing things of little value. The majority of the Louisiana Supreme Court justices saw no reason to take another look at Bryant's case.

OFFENDERS TREATED DIFFERENTLY

Bernette J. Johnson was the first Black justice on the Louisiana Supreme Court. She was also the only justice who supported a review of Bryant's case. She wrote her opinion about Bryant's situation. She said the laws that led to Bryant's punishment were linked to slavery and racism. The Civil War (1861–1865) ended slavery in the United States. In the years that followed, many

THE BLACK MAJORITY

Habitual offender laws affect Black defendants more than those of any other race. Almost 80 percent of the people serving habitual offender sentences in Louisiana are Black. But Black people make up just 32.8 percent of the state's population. The law is much more likely to affect Black people.

The Louisiana Supreme Court building is in New Orleans.

LIKELIHOOD OF
IMPRISONMENT

These images show how likely it is for men and women of various races who were born in 2001 to be imprisoned at some point in their lives. What do you notice about the image? How does it help you understand the text?

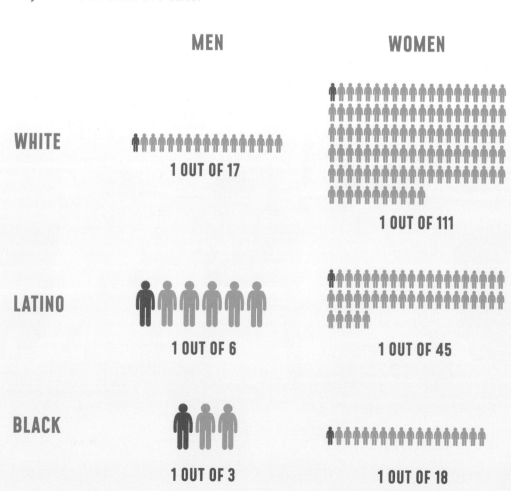

MEN | WOMEN

WHITE

1 OUT OF 17

1 OUT OF 111

LATINO

1 OUT OF 6

1 OUT OF 45

BLACK

1 OUT OF 3

1 OUT OF 18

Signs in segregated regions indicated the spaces people of color had to use.

Southern states made new laws. The laws kept Black people at a disadvantage. Johnson said poverty often drives people to commit petty crimes. Laws that give excessive punishments for petty crimes often target Black offenders. Many Black people have less wealth than white people. In many cases this is because of discrimination and racism.

Things did change for Bryant in October 2020. The Louisiana Committee on Parole voted unanimously for his release. This meant he would serve the rest of his sentence in the community. He could find a job. But he would still be supervised.

The United States has a long history of treating Black people differently than white people. And this is still a problem today. Black defendants often receive longer sentences than white defendants. Some people who commit minor offenses lose certain rights. Racism isn't limited to the criminal justice system. Separating people by race is known as segregation. At one time this practice was common in the United States. Outright segregation is no longer legal. But there are still systems that cause many Black people to live and work separately from white people. This often leads to unfair treatment. Racism continues to be a problem in the United States.

STRAIGHT TO THE
SOURCE

Racial disparities exist throughout the justice system. Black and Hispanic youths are more likely than white youths to be tried as adults in court. LaDoris Cordell served as a judge in Santa Clara County in California. In an interview, she explained how to address this disparity:

> One way is to increase the number of judges on the bench who are judges who look like the people who come before them. So . . . they are less likely to engage in that kind of stereotyping when some young kid who is of the same background or same ethnic background comes before that judge. . . . The other is, there are judges who are white, black, whatever, who have those biases. The idea is to address those biases, to get them to address it, which means judicial training.

Source: "Is the System Racially Biased?" *PBS Frontline*, n.d., pbs.org. Accessed 7 Oct. 2020.

BACK IT UP

Cordell is using evidence to support a point. Write a paragraph describing the point Cordell is making. Then write down two or three pieces of evidence used to make the point.

FROM SLAVERY TO UNPAID LABOR

The United States has a long history with slavery. Beginning in the 1500s, Spanish settlers kidnapped or bought people from Africa's West Coast. The Spanish brought these people to what is now Florida. In 1619 the slave trade to the American colonies began. European settlers brought Africans to Jamestown in what is now Virginia. The enslaved people were sold to white settlers. The settlers made the enslaved people work on their farms and in their homes.

A historical image shows an enslaved father being sold and separated from his family. Historical images often used stereotypes of people of color.

A historical image shows enslaved people working on a cotton plantation.

The white settlers saw the Black people as their property. Enslaved people were not allowed to come and go freely. They weren't allowed to learn to read or write. They weren't given privacy from slaveholders. The slaveholders called themselves the slaves' masters. Enslaved people who did not do what they were told were punished. This often meant being beaten or whipped. By the late 1700s, the US Constitution defined a slave as three-fifths of a person for the purpose of counting state populations.

Owners of large plantations depended heavily on slave labor. These large farms were in the Southern states. Common crops included cotton and sugar. Eventually some members of the government wanted to end slavery. The Southern states resisted. They did not want to lose their unpaid labor. Unpaid labor had made many slaveholders rich. For this reason several Southern states withdrew from the country. This led to the Civil War. The war ended slavery. In 1865 the Thirteenth Amendment to the Constitution made

HOLDING BLACK PEOPLE BACK

Some laws made it tough for Black people to find good jobs. Some laws said that a Black worker could not start a new job without permission from his or her last employer. This made it easy for an employer to mistreat Black employees. The employer could refuse to let an employee start a new job. The employee could not find new work.

President Abraham Lincoln supported the Thirteenth Amendment.

slavery illegal. It was a huge victory for Black Americans. But it was not the end of their mistreatment.

UNPAID LABOR

The Thirteenth Amendment outlawed slavery. But it had a loophole. The amendment said judges could sentence a person convicted of a crime to hard labor. This affected Black people more than white people.

Many former slaveholders saw an opportunity. People who had lost their slaves could still get cheap labor. The government would simply lease the convicts to business owners. Plantations, coal mines, and railroad companies all paid the government for the cheap labor. Black men, women, and even children could be forced to work if they were found guilty of crimes. Many white people made laws called Black Codes. These laws targeted Black people. The laws increased the number of Black people

PERSPECTIVES
SLAVE DEBT
Some Black Codes offered an option other than forced labor. Sometimes the offender could pay a fine instead. But this wasn't an option for most newly freed slaves. Few had enough money for the fines. So they were forced to work. In this way, many white people kept Black people indebted to them. Douglas A. Blackmon wrote the book *Slavery by Another Name*. Blackmon writes that arresting, selling, and delivering Black people to workplaces was common. Official documents did a poor job of hiding that the crimes were exaggerated. "Repeatedly," he says, "the timing and scale of surges in arrests appeared more attuned to rise and dips in the need for cheap labor than any [clearly shown] acts of crime."

Children convicted of crimes could be sent to work on farms.

convicted of crimes. This meant there were more cheap laborers.

In parts of Louisiana, a Black person could not go anywhere without a permit from an employer. Breaking this law could mean four days of labor. Many new laws gave harsh punishments for small offenses.

In Mississippi any theft over ten dollars in value was considered grand larceny. This is the theft of valuable property. The crime carries a higher penalty than stealing things of low value. Southern states also began hiring more police officers. They could arrest more people. On paper, slavery had ended. But in reality white people had found ways to keep Black people enslaved.

FURTHER EVIDENCE

Chapter Two discusses how Black people were mistreated after the Thirteenth Amendment. What was one of this chapter's main points? What evidence is included to support this point? Read the article at the website below. Does the information on the website support this point? Does it present new evidence?

THE STORY OF CONVICT LEASING IN FLORIDA

abdocorelibrary.com/history-of-racism

KEEPING BLACK PEOPLE DOWN

I n 1870 the Fifteenth Amendment gave Black men the right to vote. In another 50 years, the Nineteenth Amendment gave that right to women. These amendments meant people could not be kept from voting because of race or gender. But they did not guarantee the ability to vote. Even today's discussion about women's voting rights focuses mainly on white women. Some people are working to make the stories of Black women who fought for their own rights

Women gained the right to vote in 1920. But that right was sometimes only extended to white women.

23

RULES FOR VOTING

Southern states had several requirements for Black people who wanted to vote. Voters had to live in a state for one or two years. This negatively affected people of color who lived in cities. They moved around frequently. People convicted of a felony or certain other crimes also could not vote. The selected crimes were ones that Black people were most prosecuted for. Many formerly enslaved people could not read and write. In Louisiana, people who could not read and write needed to own property of a certain value in order to vote.

common knowledge. The book *Vanguard* by Martha S. Jones was published in 2020. It told these women's stories.

Black voters were more likely to strike down legislation that racist politicians and voters supported. White people in power made laws to keep people of color from voting. Several Southern states passed such laws. They said that a man could vote only if his grandfather had held the right before 1867. This posed

A historical illustration shows Black men voting in the late 1800s.

no issue for most white voters. But no Black people were allowed to vote before 1870. This law made it impossible for Black men to vote.

A person who can read and write is literate. White people in certain states made literacy tests. Some lawmakers said the tests were to ensure Black people could read. They said the ability to read was important for casting an informed vote. But these tests were just another way to limit the rights of Black people. Many former slaves did not know how to read. And many cities and towns rigged the tests. White officials gave Black voters a difficult test. White voters received an easy one.

Former slaves often had less money than white people. Few earned good wages. For this reason, some states made poll taxes. Most white voters could afford these fees. But the fees were just high enough to keep most Black people from voting.

In the 1960s people around the country marched to protest the policies that kept people of color in some regions from voting.

These attempts to limit the rights of Black people are often called Jim Crow laws. Jim Crow was a fictional Black character. He was from minstrel shows of the early 1800s. These live shows featured white actors in

Schools for Black students were often lower quality than those attended by white students.

dark makeup. They pretended to be Black people. The shows used insulting stereotypes of Black people.

SEGREGATION

Racism did not exist only in the southern states. White people throughout the country tried to limit Black people. White people in some places supported segregation. They said it created separate but equal settings. But there was nothing equal about it.

SEGREGATION LAWS
IN 1953

Segregation in public places was required by law in 17 states in 1953. The practice was outlawed in 16 states. The remaining states either allowed it in some cases or had no laws about it. How does this help you understand the importance of ending segregation?

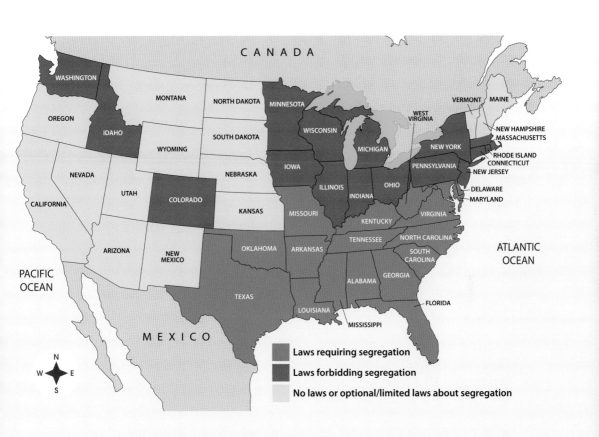

Black and white families were not allowed to worship in the same churches. Black and white students could not attend the same schools. Some businesses would not serve Black people. Signs that read "White only" were common. The businesses that did allow Black customers had separate spaces for them. Signs in hotels, restaurants, and theaters labeled these areas. Black people had to sit at the backs of buses. They could not use the same drinking fountains as white people.

Segregation was widely accepted for many years. Then the civil rights era began in the 1950s. More and more people thought segregation was unfair. They spoke out against it. Protests against racism became more common over the next decade. Lawsuits challenged segregation. A historic Supreme Court case happened in 1954. It was called *Brown v. Board of Education of Topeka.* It outlawed segregation in schools. Ten years later the Civil Rights Act of 1964 ended segregation in public places. It also made racial employment discrimination illegal. But the fight for equal treatment continues.

EXPLORE ONLINE

Chapter Three discusses school segregation. Watch the video at the website below. How is the information from this source the same as the information in Chapter Three? What new information did you learn from the article?

BROWN V. BOARD OF EDUCATION OF TOPEKA
abdocorelibrary.com/history-of-racism

STRIPPED OF RIGHTS

Many people think that racism is a thing of the past. But people of color are still treated differently under US law than white people. One example can be seen in prison sentences. Black people make up 13 percent of the US population. But they make up 33 percent of prisoners. White people make up 63 percent of the US population. But they are just 30 percent of prisoners. This shows an inequality in the justice system.

Black people are imprisoned at a higher rate than white people.

FEWER PRISONERS

More than 2.3 million people are currently serving time in US prisons. Keeping all these people incarcerated is expensive. It costs billions of dollars each year. Policies that keep people in prison longer affect people outside prison too. These policies have negative economic consequences for the whole society. Sentencing laws that incarcerate people of different races at the same rate could decrease the populations in prisons by nearly 40 percent.

It also shows inequalities in society that increase the risk of Black people ending up in the criminal justice system. Nearly 19 percent of Black people lived in poverty in 2019. Just 7.3 percent of white people lived in poverty. And 62 percent of Black people live in neighborhoods with violent crime. Children exposed to violence are at higher risk of developing mental health issues. Exposure to violence also makes children more likely to commit crimes as adults.

Current practices in law enforcement contribute to the disparity. Black and white Americans use illegal drugs at similar rates. But Black people are almost four times more likely to be arrested for drug-related offenses. And in courts, Black people are more likely to be charged as habitual offenders than white people who had similar offenses.

When people are arrested, courts often allow them to post bail. This means that people can pay money to stay out of jail until they appear in court. People who are poor cannot always afford to pay bail. Black people are more than two times more likely to live in poverty than white people. Many Black defendants are unable to post bail to leave jail.

This was the case for Lavette Mayes of Chicago, Illinois. Mayes was arrested after a physical fight with her mother-in-law. It was her first arrest. But a judge set her bail at $250,000. She did not have enough money to pay it. She stayed in jail for the next 14 months. By the

time Mayes got out of jail, she had served more time than she would have been required to for being found guilty. She lost her job and her housing as a result.

People are also policed differently based on their race. ABC News looked at arrest data from 2018. It found that Black people in 800 US jurisdictions were five times more likely to be arrested than white people. A jurisdiction is the area a court has control over. In some areas Black people were ten times more likely to be arrested. Experts think unfair practices such as racial profiling play a role. This is when bias leads officers to target people of certain races more heavily. They are more likely to suspect people of some races of crimes. It leads to more traffic stops of Black people. Stop-and-frisk programs also lead to a higher rate of Black people being arrested. This practice is when police stop people they think have committed or will commit crimes. Police often target young Black and

Lavette Mayes, *center*, has spoken at events about how incarceration affected her life and her children's lives.

PERSPECTIVES

POLITICAL ADVANTAGE

Jeffery Robinson is a deputy legal director for the American Civil Liberties Union. In an article, he wrote, "In many . . . states, incarcerated people are stripped of their vote but remain counted as part of the populations . . . where they are locked up, boosting the electoral advantage of those districts." Some people believe states do not want to include prisoners in the voting process. But they want the prisoners' numbers to help their region get a bigger say in national issues. Population determines how many representatives each state gets in Congress. It also decides how many electoral votes each state gets in presidential elections.

Hispanic men and boys. They stop people to check if those people are carrying weapons.

LOSING VOTING RIGHTS

One important right an American has is the right to vote. Voting gives people a voice in their government. Each vote counts. But in many states, people convicted of crimes lose their voting rights. Some lose the right while they are serving time. Some lose the right permanently. In 21 states people

In 2019 Florida granted people convicted of a felony the right to vote. But it required that the felons pay back what they owed to the courts first.

cannot vote if they are on probation or parole.

Probation is a period of time after a prisoner is released. Breaking certain rules during this time means the person will go back to prison. In 11 states someone convicted of a felony can never vote again. Black people are given a higher rate of mandatory minimum sentences than white people. This means their voting rights are taken away for longer lengths of time, if they are ever returned.

Before the Civil War, voting was not linked to whether a person had been convicted of a crime in most states. But between 1865 and 1880, 13 states passed disenfranchisement laws. These are laws that strip the voting rights of a person convicted of a crime. In 1965 Congress passed the Voting Rights Act. It made discriminatory voting practices illegal. But disenfranchisement laws continue to keep many Black people from voting. Many people say these laws uphold racism.

Nothing can be done to change the racism of the past. But by learning about the history of racism in the United States, Americans can better understand the present and improve the future.

STRAIGHT TO THE
SOURCE

Robert D. Crutchfield and Gregory A. Weeks wrote an article about policing drug crimes. The authors said that Black or Latino people do not commit more of these crimes than white people. They explained:

> Some observers have claimed that African American and Latino drug dealers are more likely to be arrested because their activities are more likely to occur in open air public drug markets than does the dealing of whites. But at least one study has found that police [choose] to pursue open air drug markets with minority dealers and ignore those where whites are selling. Overall, the war on drugs has been especially hard on minority individuals and communities, and this cannot be justified by overrepresentation of these groups in this particular form of criminal behavior.

Source: Robert D. Crutchfield and Gregory A. Weeks. "The Effects of Mass Incarceration on Communities of Color." *Issues in Science and Technology*, vol. XXXII no. 1, Fall 2015, issues.org. Accessed 3 Sept. 2020.

WHAT'S THE BIG IDEA?

Take a close look at this passage. What connections did the authors make between the ways police treat people of color and white people?

IMPORTANT DATES

1865
The Thirteenth Amendment to the US Constitution outlaws slavery.

1870
The Fifteenth Amendment grants Black men the right to vote, but Black Codes and then later Jim Crow Laws aim to keep them from doing so.

1920
The Nineteenth Amendment gives women the right to vote, but women of color still face barriers to voting.

1954
The US Supreme Court rules that segregating schools is unconstitutional.

1964
Congress passes the Civil Rights Act of 1964.

1965
Congress passes the Voting Rights Act of 1965.

1997
Fair Wayne Bryant is arrested for stealing a pair of hedge clippers. He receives a life sentence for the crime. Bryant was released on parole in October 2020.

STOP AND THINK

Surprise Me

This book discusses the history of racism in America. After reading this book, what two or three facts about racism did you find most surprising? Write a few sentences about each fact. Why did you find each fact surprising?

You Are There

Chapter Four talks about voter disenfranchisement. Imagine your class is voting on where to go for a field trip. But the teacher will not let you vote because you were talking in class. Write a letter to your principal about how this makes you feel. Be sure to add plenty of details.

Take a Stand

This book discusses disenfranchisement. Do you think people in prison should be able to vote? What about people who have been charged with a felony and have already served time for the crime? Explain your stance, offering evidence for your opinion.

GLOSSARY

appeal
a legal action that asks the courts to reassess a verdict

convict
to find someone guilty of a crime

defendant
someone accused of a crime

disparity
a big difference

felony
a serious crime

incarcerate
to imprison a person for a crime

loophole
an unclear part of a law or other binding text that allows the rule in the text to be avoided

mandatory minimum sentence
the smallest punishment required by law

parole
the release of a prisoner before completion of a sentence

sentence
a punishment handed down by a judge or court

stereotype
a simplification about a large and complex category

ONLINE RESOURCES

To learn more about the history of racism in America, visit our free resource websites below.

Visit **abdocorelibrary.com** or scan this QR code for free Common Core resources for teachers and students, including vetted activities, multimedia, and booklinks, for deeper subject comprehension.

Visit **abdobooklinks.com** or scan this QR code for free additional online weblinks for further learning. These links are routinely monitored and updated to provide the most current information available.

LEARN MORE

Harris, Duchess. *Two Bloody Sundays*. Abdo Publishing, 2019.

Harris, Duchess, and Blythe Lawrence. *Daisy Bates and the Little Rock Nine*. Abdo Publishing, 2019.

ABOUT THE
AUTHORS

Duchess Harris, JD, PhD

Dr. Harris is a professor of American Studies and Political Science at Macalester College and curator of the Duchess Harris Collection of ABDO books. She is also the coauthor of the collection, which features popular titles such as *Hidden Human Computers: The Black Women of NASA* and series including Freedom's Promise and Race and American Law. In addition, Dr. Harris hosts the *Freedom's Promise* podcast with her son.

Before working with ABDO, Dr. Harris authored several other books on the topics of race, culture, and American history. She served as an associate editor for *Litigation News*, the American Bar Association Section of Litigation's quarterly flagship publication, and was the first editor in chief of *Law Raza*, an interactive online journal covering race and the law, published at William Mitchell College of Law. She has earned a BA in History from the University of Pennsylvania, a PhD in American Studies from the University of Minnesota, and a JD from William Mitchell College of Law.

Tammy Gagne

Tammy Gagne has written dozens of books for both adults and children. Her recent titles include *Justice for George Floyd* and *Race and the Media in Modern America*. She lives in northern New England with her husband and son.

INDEX